W9-DEC-711

FJORDS vol. I

Also by Zachary Schomburg:

The Man Suit
Scary, No Scary

FJORDS vol.1

by Zachary Schomburg

Black Ocean
Boston · New York · Chicago

Black Ocean
P.O. Box 52030
Boston, MA 02205
blackocean.org

Cover image by Zachary Schomburg & Denny Schmickle
Book design by Janaka Stucky

ISBN 978-0-9844752-5-4

Library of Congress Cataloging-in-Publication Data

Schomburg, Zachary, 1977-
  Fjords / Zachary Schomburg.
    p. cm.
  Poems, some previously published in a chapbook, or journals and websites.
  ISBN 978-0-9844752-5-4
  I. Title.
  PS3619.C4536F56 2012
  811'.6–dc22

                          2011052351

Printed in Canada
FIRST EDITION

ACKNOWLEDGMENTS

Some of these poems have been published in *1110*, *Black Warrior Review*, *Caketrain*, *Columbia Poetry Review*, *Filter*, *iO*, *Jellyfish*, *Lit*, *Lumina*, *Paperbag*, *Poets.org*, *Poor Claudia*, *Portland Review*, *Provincetown Arts*, *Salt Hill*, *Sixth Finch*, *Tin House*, and *Zero Ducats*.

A chapbook, *From the Fjords*, which included some of these poems, was published by Spork Press in 2010.

"Magazine Stand" is after a narrative from Jean-Luc Godard's *Vivre sa Vie*. "Death Letter" begins with a version of a line from Son House's "Death Letter Blues." "The Search" is after a poem by Mary Ruefle titled "The Butcher's Story."

Some of these poems are for the following people: Molly Brodak, Heather Christle, Lisa Ciccarello, Steve Dawson, Tyler Allan Ferrin, Emily Kendal Frey, Janey Gibilisco, A. Minetta Gould, Remy Jewell, Natasha Kessler, Jesse Lichtenstein, Joseph Mains, Kyle Morton, Todd Pangilinan, Bruce Schomburg, Brandon Shimoda, Mathias Svalina, Drew Swenhaugen, James Tate, and Nancy Wong.

CONTENTS

What Would Kill Me 1

Fjords of Deaths 2

The Wild Meaninglessness 3

Falling in Love with the
  Death Thought 4

The Fake Sleeping Scare 5

Because It Comes Right
  at You Does Not Mean
  It Comes to Save You 6

Beautiful Island 7

Terrible Deer 8

Airplane 9

Lake 10

First Time in Paris 11

Magazine Stand 12

The Difference Between
  Sadness and Suffering 13

Someone Falls in Love
  with Someone 14

The Animal Spell 15

Death Letter 16

Unkind Swans 17

Meat Counter 18

The Woman Who Falls
  From the Sky 19

The Fire is Out of Control
  and We Are Almost Dead 20

Movie Theater 21

The Feelings. 22
New Dress Shirt. 23
Squirrel Problem 24
Black Angel of Death. 25
Breath-Holding Championship 26
New Job Serving Fried Pies 27
Refrigerator General 28
Large Refrigerator of the Valley 29
Testy Pony. 30
Staring Problem 31
Lost Forest of Nakai. 32
The Person Who Was
   Expected. 33
I Had a Baby with a Woman
   the Other day. 34
The People with Arms 35
Behind a Wall of Animals 36
Tiny Castle 37
A Life in Space. 38
Miner Death. 39
I Love Your Fighting Style 40
The One About the Robbers 41
The Donut Hawk. 42
Don't Step on the Frog 43
After Taking Out the
   Garbage for the First Time. 44
The Search 45
Fishing for Stingrays. 46
I Climbed a Mountain and
   Fucked it into the Sea. 47

Hands. 48
Costa Rica 49
Building of Unseen Cats 50
The Killing Trees 51
Neighborhood Plague 52
Leaving the House 53
I am the Dead Person
 Inside Me 54
Casting Out the King
 of Boys 55
What I Did with the Rock 56
The Reckoner. 57

Index

WHAT WOULD KILL ME

From the very beginning I knew exactly what would
kill me. Regardless, I convinced myself that it could
be anything. I convinced myself that what would
kill me would be made up of any of the random
things that would kill anybody else. When I walked
my dog around the neighborhood, I saw what
would kill me hovering in the trees. When I swam
in the ocean, I felt what would kill me nudging at
my ankles. At the grocery store: behind the cereal
boxes. I grew old like this, seeing what would kill
me on my dinner plates, in the rabbit cages. I grew
old distracting myself from what I knew to be true.
And then, just like I knew it would, it came late one
night, booming with slowness, from the fjords.

FJORDS OF DEATHS

There is a place in this world where my deaths live, on the west coast of Spitsbergen. They thawed from the steep cliff walls the same day I was born. They bide their time in the endless silent sunlight, making up beautiful songs that only one of them will get to sing.

THE WILD MEANINGLESSNESS

The people here have all fallen in love with their own meaninglessness, but I'm not sure what that means. I mean, what else can we do but mean? Just the other day, for example, we threw strawberries from the roof at the birds. We can't help it. I mean, we can't help anything at all. Our faces are swelling up into the realm of the poppable, then we look at our poppable faces in the glass at the aquarium, the sharks circling, and we mean away.

FALLING IN LOVE WITH THE DEATH THOUGHT

Falling in love with the death thought is a way of never really dying. You let an idea hold you in its real arms. This is how you love: you try over and over again to throw a red balloon across the river from a tree.

THE FAKE SLEEPING SCARE

The only kind of sleep I get is fake sleep. I am so fake tired all of the time. I can tell you only fake sleep too, and that you're fake tired all of the time. I can tell that you can tell I only fake sleep too, and that you know that I know that. I'm afraid we'll never make it like this to any actual ending, that we'll just keep on living forever after everyone gives up and goes home. *You're not my enemy* I say as you fake sleep, but you are.

BECAUSE IT COMES RIGHT AT YOU DOES NOT MEAN IT COMES TO SAVE YOU

My father and I are lost in the Arctic Ocean when we spot a boat tearing toward us through the crust. I am on his shoulders, my feet black like cold tar. When the boat gets closer, he sets me down on the ice and we hold hands. *Do you think it has come to save us?* I ask. *Well, it is coming right at us* my father says. But as it gets closer, it does not slow down. *It is not slowing down* I say. It is unbearably loud, an angry comet in a bright white universe, a terrible ice-splitting machine. When it gets too close, we panic and let go of each other's hands. We dive out of the way in opposite directions. Chunks of ice are thrown around our bodies. When the landscape settles again, the boat is a silent grey eye on the horizon. There is a new icy rivulet between my father and me. My father is face down in the white on the other side of the rivulet, a frozen obedience. I want to yell *I do not regret you* but I am just a little boy. Sons do not give birth to their fathers. There is no regret without birth. And there is no spring— all these years and no real spring and no real death.

BEAUTIFUL ISLAND

The boat has come to pick me up. When I pass the island, I wave so vigorously that my hand falls off into the sea. I am becoming so beautiful, my body shedding into the scenery, my blood pumping wildly. Everyone on the island is so beautiful, how they are missing every part of their body. There is so much blood in the trees. It will be easy to fall in love like this.

TERRIBLE DEER

I am in a hospital bed when I feel an overwhelming pain in my stomach. I am sure I am going to die if I don't get any help. *Nurse! Nurse!* I yell, but no nurse comes. There are no signs of any nurses. There are no signs of any other patients. There are no signs that electricity has been invented. There is no glass in the windows. I get up from the bed and walk slowly out into the corridor. Some papers are swept up in a breeze across the floor. *Someone please help me! My water broke!* My pleas echo in the corridor and then it finally happens. The terrible deer that has been clawing and biting at my insides for years crashes out of me and spills onto the tiles. It then quickly leaps into the night through the window. I can hear it dash through the bushes. I can hear it splash into the ocean. I can hear it tear at the air in the sky. It is the world's problem now.

AIRPLANE

I am asleep on an airplane when I hear a loud explosion. The nose of the airplane is suddenly pointed downward and the wings are on fire. Entire families are crawling on the ceiling but everything is completely silent. The fire is silently eating the luggage. Everyone's mouths are open but I can't hear any screaming. I think maybe I lost my hearing. I want to test it out so I scream *I love you! I love you!* They are the only words I can think of to scream. Outside the window I see my house. My dad mowing the lawn. A little boy walking a dog.

LAKE

I dive into the lake and cut my chest open on a piece of broken glass. The giant shard of glass goes through my chest and out of my back. When I stand up out of the water I look like a statue in a blood fountain. The only person on shore who can hear me is a woman with a baby. *Here, take my baby* she says, and she walks into the water and hands me her baby. *But I'm bleeding to death* I say. *But it's for you* she says.

FIRST TIME IN PARIS

I wake up in Paris. I am on the top of the Eiffel Tower. Children and their mothers are speaking French there. *Am I in Paris?* I ask. All of the mothers laugh at me and then all of the children laugh alongside their mothers. *I've never been to Paris before* I said. They laugh harder. When I look over the edge, I see that you are crawling up the tower, your eyes small and vengeful. With all of your might, you rock the tower back and forth. It tips up on its iron legs—it bends at its hinges. The children and their mothers stop laughing and start panicking. Without hesitation, for the good of us all, I put my boot to your face and kick you off to your death. You look like a tattered bouquet of flowers falling. Everyone except for me cheers, but in French. As you bleed into the stone streets, I know exactly how much I love you—I can almost measure it. Now I have to save myself, and I have to save everyone else. It is so important to kill, to save. They are sometimes the same thing. So then I pick up one of the children.

MAGAZINE STAND

I was flipping through magazines at the magazine
stand when 1000 francs fell from a woman's purse.
I put my foot on her 1000 francs, hoping she would
walk away. She did walk away, but then came back
to look at me, right into my eyes, as if she was look-
ing for her lost money there. I almost said so many
things, and I could see that she almost said so many
things. I could tell that at one exact point in the
future we are both swans in the same pond
wrapping our long black necks around each other
until it hurts.

THE DIFFERENCE BETWEEN SADNESS AND SUFFERING

The world became a bag of seeds. This is no one's fault. Nothing is anyone's fault, which is something we must remember. The world is just a bag of seeds, and there is nowhere for the seeds to be planted. This is the prayer I came up with before dinner at your mom's house. *What is this a prayer for?* she asked. *I don't know. Maybe it is a prayer for your daughter* I said. Then I told everybody at the table that the difference between sadness and suffering is where the love comes from. We think we've figured it out, and then it is a fist that comes exploding from our eyes.

SOMEONE FALLS IN LOVE WITH SOMEONE

Someone falls in love with someone but that person falls in love with someone else, and that person falls in love with a different person, and that person falls in love with someone else too. I am the third person and you are the fourth person. I am an ambulance driver and you are an ambulance driver. I am resuscitating someone in a basement and you are resuscitating someone else in the same basement. *Are you falling in love with someone else?* I ask from across the basement but you can't hear me. I am being strangled by the asphyxiated person who I am resuscitating and you are being strangled by the asphyxiated person who you are resuscitating. I hope this is it. I hope we all die just like this, in someone else's arms, young and beautiful and true.

THE ANIMAL SPELL

Someone once told me that animals are people under spells, and if you fall in love with them the spell will be lifted. I recently fell in love with a black trumpeter swan. I watched her ruffle her neck feathers for hours, watched her peck bugs from her breast. I was sure she would make a beautiful bride, but she was always a black trumpeter swan. I once brushed a horse's hair for 3 straight years until it crumpled into death. The truth is there is no such thing as spells. The world is always as it is, and always as it seems. And love is just our own kind voice that we whisper into our own blood.

DEATH LETTER

I get a letter in the morning that said the woman I love is dead, that she has been trampled by elephants. I haven't seen her in years, but I think about her every time I make the bed, every time I set the table. I think about how perfect we would have been together. When I arrive at her house with flowers to pay my respects, I see her in the window, dusting the sill. She isn't dead at all. She shows no signs of being trampled, even her clothes are starched and pressed. I knock on the door and she opens it. *You're not dead* I say. *Who are you?* she says. *What do you mean?* I say. *It's me.* But her eyes just squint at me as if I were microscopic. *Weren't you trampled by elephants?* I say. *No* she says. *There aren't even any elephants around here.* When I walk away, flowers in my fist, I think about all the different kinds of death. I wish she would have been dead just like the letter said. There is more truth in that kind of death, and I felt so much closer to her then.

UNKIND SWANS

The unkind swans were about to hatch from their gigantic swan eggs. Everybody from the village came to watch the eggs shake and then crack, but day after day, the eggs only shook and never cracked. The villagers made room in their busy days, even skipped their daily chores to watch the hatching, but the hatching never came. Only shaking. I knew this was the unkind swans' first act of unkindness. In the middle of the night, when everyone in the village was asleep, I carried the gigantic swan eggs to the cliff, one at a time, and threw them off. I threw them off to save us all. But when they cracked onto the earth below, what was inside looked incredibly kind, like wet strawberries in the dirt. O to shake forever in a shell.

MEAT COUNTER

I wake up inside the meat counter of my grandfather's grocery store. I am shivering, surrounded by parsley. When my fingers touch the glass, they make blood smudges. I hear my grandfather speaking to a customer. They are both laughing and I can see their pants. The customer tells my grandfather, *I'll take his leg*. I touch my palm to the glass and leave a red palm print before my grandfather picks me up, gently like a baby, and begins to saw me into parts on the meat saw. He breaks my neck and cuts my head off, then breaks my leg and pulls it from my hip. I try to tell him it's me. I think our eyes meet, for just a millisecond, but I can't be sure.

THE WOMAN WHO FALLS FROM THE SKY

I am at a fruit stand on the side of the road when a woman falls from the sky onto a pile of cantaloupe. She has French braids and is not dead. This is how everyday starts with us, a kind of waking up into the day in front of me, and then every night she falls through a dark hole. I should say this isn't exactly true, the part about falling through the sky. The truth is we woke up like the rest of you, in a bed with our hot mouths falling open. But it was glorious, a goddamned miracle, the crashing into and the never dying.

THE FIRE IS OUT OF CONTROL
AND WE ARE ALMOST DEAD

The game we play is to suffer miserably in a fire. We can't control the fire. We can't control the future where the fire is waiting, and we can't control the present, where the fire is everywhere and eating our insides. We can only control the past. It's where our bodies still are, moving so freely, not on fire, looking for the hurt dog under all the porches and afraid to find it. *Do you want to play again?* you ask. *No I don't want to play again* I say.

MOVIE THEATER

I am working in the ticket booth of the movie theater when you come in and take off my pants. You are very turned on. You start to take off your pants too until we are both standing there in the darkness of the ticket booth, our pants at our ankles. Neither of us is wearing any underwear. The people in line outside the ticket booth keep asking for tickets because the movie is about to start. *I can't do this* I tell you. *Because the movie is going to start?* you ask. *No* I say *because I just got done having sex with someone named Barbara.* When you walk away, you walk away into a lake so salty it looks like milk. You become a boat with mint candy for skin.

THE FEELINGS

I had a difficult dinner with the feelings. We sat at the far ends of the table and looked down. I wanted to pop a red balloon or put my head in the ceiling fan. *What has become of us?* I asked. I went to bed, and the feelings stayed up watching television on the couch. In the morning, the feelings were gone, an empty bag of chips on the floor, my shoes missing. A few weeks later, I got a blank postcard from Paris. I thought this must be how Paris feels, like it could burn itself down, like it just can't take itself any more, like it is out of words, out of days to move forward into. I walked to the grocery store and I thought I saw the feelings there buying things.

NEW DRESS SHIRT

The first time I wear my new dress shirt, the woman at the bank tells me how well it fits on my torso, how it lights up my eyes, that my eyes can light a dark room, make night into day, etc. I decide I will never take off my new dress shirt. It is the beginning of a new life for me, a life of being noticed, of reaping reward. With my new dress shirt on, I will run for mayor uncontested. I will marry the woman at the bank, perhaps after saving her from a vicious attack by a desperate man-eating lion. But when it happens at the bank, when the lion crashes through the drive-thru teller window, my new dress shirt hugging my torso perfectly, I stand paralyzed while the new love of my life is torn apart and eaten, a shredded pants suit hanging like a bath towel from the lion's blood-stained incisors, bloody deposit slips pasted to the lion's wet paws. I am almost certain I see that lion look at my new dress shirt, at how well it fits.

SQUIRREL PROBLEM

I watch a squirrel get run over by a car on my walk to work. She is lying dead in the street and still has an acorn in her little hands. I am amazed at how she is able to hold on to her acorn after being tumbled like that, after bouncing so high off the street. I walk over to the squirrel and see that her face is blown to bits and looks like uncased sausage spilling onto the asphalt. But that acorn is still so tight in her hands. I pick her up by her tail, take off my dress shirt and swaddle her in it, then put her in my bag. I know right where she is as I walk into work, everybody looking at me, everybody asking me about my shirtlessness. The world is as steady as if it were sewn into the skin of the universe.

BLACK ANGEL OF DEATH

I was in bed when the black angel of death flew into my room from the open window and started kissing me on the neck. It felt like a bag of jagged rocks. Her soft belly was shaking as she laughed, all those black shining jewels. I don't know how best to tell you about the angel, about what death really is. It seems so implausible until it happens. You start to sweat and you get swallowed into the dark. Then you're swinging on a rope over a beautiful cliff, only there's no such thing as beauty.

BREATH-HOLDING CHAMPIONSHIP

I surprise everyone with my exceptional performance in the breath-holding championship. Around the 8-minute mark, my last remaining opponent drops to his knees and struggles for a breath. The paramedics rush to his side, oxygen masks in their shaky hands. Even after I pass the world record mark, I am calm, stronger than ever. I just stand there in front of the audience, not breathing, while the clock ticks and ticks. Despite my calmness, the audience panics. They cover the eyes of their children. *This isn't possible* they yell. *He should be dead. Breathe, just breathe!* But I don't need a breath. They're going to kill me in order to save their own understanding of how the world works, or they're going to go home. Either way, I'm not breathing until everything unravels back into blood and string.

NEW JOB SERVING FRIED PIES

It is my first day serving fried pies out of a trailer. I am part of a four-person operation. There is one person who makes the pies, one person who puts the pies in a vat of grease, one person who takes the money, and me. It is my job to sprinkle powdered sugar on the pies and put them in a wrapper. Before long, the other three are dead, bleeding in a pile on the trailer floor. There is a very long line of impatient customers. It looks like a kite string curling off into the distance. *I want a chocolate pie* one of them says. I look around at all the strange machines just sitting there like a family that had just adopted me. *Can't you see we're dying?* I said.

REFRIGERATOR GENERAL

I am wrapped only in a wet towel when the refrigerator general knocks on my door. *I need to inspect your refrigerator* he says. *You can't just go around inspecting people's refrigerators* I say, the cold air from the door on my flushed thighs. *But, ma'am, I'm the refrigerator general* he says. *Well, may I see your identification?* I ask. The refrigerator general digs around in his breast pocket and pulls out a card designed to look a little like a refrigerator. *That's very clever but I'm not sure it proves anything* I say. *Ma'am* he says with urgency. He pushes open the door a little and steps inside. *But I'm in my towel* I say. *Relax, ma'am, I'm a professional* he says from the kitchen. *But I don't even have a refrigerator* I say. *Just as I suspected* he says. I stand completely motionless in the corner of the kitchen and start humming. He stops writing his citation and stares at me, eyes like a bat's eyes. *Ma'am?* he asks. *Ma'am?* the blood draining from his face. He tugs gently on my towel and looks inside. I can see it in his eyes, how he wants me to be something human.

LARGE REFRIGERATOR OF THE VALLEY

I come down from the mountains carrying heavy refrigerator parts on my back, and I build a very large refrigerator. It is the largest refrigerator ever built, roughly fifteen to twenty times the size of an average refrigerator. *I have built a very large refrigerator* I announce to one woman who lives in a shack by the river. *You may put anything you want in it* I say. The woman who lives in the shack appears skeptical. *Does it look like I have anything to refrigerate?* she asks. *Maybe not now* I say *but perhaps you could see the large refrigerator as a way to change your life.* The woman who lives in a shack stares for a while, her face like a plate. I can tell she is really thinking about how the large refrigerator could change her life. Then, slowly, it begins to happen. The woman who lives in a shack looks to the top of the refrigerator that is peeking out over the trees in the distance like a low white sun. *Owwwwwoooooooooooga owwwwwooooooga!* she howls. Change has come to the valley. *Yes, owwwwwoooooooooga* I say, my strong arms now around her waist, *owwwwwoooooooga.*

TESTY PONY

I am given a pony for my birthday, but it is the wrong kind of pony. It is the kind of pony that won't listen. It is testy. When I ask it to go left, it goes right. When I ask it to run, it sleeps on its side in the tall grass. So when I ask it to jump us over the river into the field I have never been to before, I have every reason to believe it will fail, that we will be swept down the river to our deaths. It is a fate for which I am prepared because the blame of our death will rest with the testy pony, and with that, I will be remembered with reverence, and the pony will be remembered with great anger. But the testy pony rears and approaches the river with unfettered bravery. Its leap is glorious. It clears the river with ease, not even getting its pony hooves wet. And then there we are on the other side of the river, the sun going down, the pony circling, looking for something to eat in the dirt. Real trust is to do so in the clear face of doubt, and to trust is to love. This is my failure, and for this I cannot be forgiven.

STARING PROBLEM

A woman walks into a room. I am in a different
room. *What has happened to your eyes?* she asks.

LOST FOREST OF NAKAI

I ask a woman for directions to The Lost Forest of Nakai. Just like I'm told, I go straight for a long while, then I take two lefts before taking two quick rights, but I never come to the wooden bridge shaped like a shoehorn. In fact, I am back where I started, but where I started is my childhood living room: a golden milk-sour carpet, my parents young on the couch. *Do you know how to get to The Lost Forest of Nakai?* I ask. My parents point down the hallway to my bedroom. When I walk in, I am on a game show blinded by lots of hot flashing lights. I am losing, and they want to hang me from a tree. *You have one final chance* they say. *Everything I have ever loved is slipping away* I say. Then some bells go off.

THE PERSON WHO WAS EXPECTED

A man is sitting at a table. A woman says *can I sit with you?* The man says *sorry, but I am expecting someone.* The woman sits down anyway and says *I am your wife.* The man says, *no, no, you're not my wife, but you do look familiar. I think I am your father.* The woman says *oh no, you're not my father, you're my son. Where have you been?* They stare at one another until the person who was expected shows up and hands the man a magic baby. It grows in his hands. Its hair spreads across the floor. This makes sense. The four of them live in the future where everything makes perfect sense under a blue crying beam of bird-light.

I HAD A BABY WITH A WOMAN THE OTHER DAY

I had a baby with a woman the other day. She looked up at me as if to ask for the time. There was no real joy or pain. The baby came out and slid into a pile of other babies. Now the pile has become so big and loud that we have no choice but to ignore it, and the air is so sad, no one can see the wild mess creeping steadily in. Everybody just keeps digging holes, then putting dead people in them, and no one even cares.

THE PEOPLE WITH ARMS

I didn't have arms. She didn't have arms. Falling in love was the easy part. We had so much to talk about, our armlessness, our being two armless citizens of such a cruel and inaccessible world. When we moved in together, the people with arms did most of our gardening, our cooking, the scrubbing in the shower. And making love was always a problem, one person with arms behind each of us, their arms reaching around our sides, doing the rubbing. If we closed our eyes, we always thought, arms were just these inconsequential things, these bendy things filled with cold blood, these things we hardly needed for love. If we closed our eyes, that kind of touching could feel right for just long enough.

BEHIND A WALL OF ANIMALS

You are behind a wall of animals tying your shoes
in the blackness. I am in front of the wall of animals
tying my shoes in the brightness. This is the world.
Trees are blooming into bright lightbulbs, and then
the lightbulbs fall and crash. The animals are
breaking into fewer animals. And our hands are
pinecones.

TINY CASTLE

I stumble upon a tiny castle in the woods. It has a tiny moat surrounding it. This is the castle where I used to live when I was tiny. The tiny king is my father and the tiny queen is my mother, but I am now too large for them to see me. I try crouching, but I can't even make myself small enough for the moat to keep me out. Once we've become large, we can never again become tiny—we can never be kept out, and we can never again be swallowed by the enormity of something besides ourselves.

A LIFE IN SPACE

You promised me we'd live in a different universe, but when we arrived, everything was the same—the gravity, the stars lined up like teeth. A woman named Barbara was there, just like the Barbara who used to live next door. She made us a layer cake for our anniversary, just like the Barbara we used to know. We could have predicted how she would run around like a piano was about to fall on her, how her eyelashes would become wires to hold all our blackness up.

MINER DEATH

This time when I come out of the mine, I step immediately into another mine. The world has finally become what I knew it would become, a series of endlessly interconnected mines. I am a thought or a disease. That is my new lot in life. You open your mouth. A bright circle of countryside is out of it.

I LOVE YOUR FIGHTING STYLE

I get into a fight with a woman who wraps her gigantic tree-trunk legs around my head so tightly that I suffer severe convulsions. I am in the hospital that night and all of my family members visit me, even the dead ones. They talk to me as if I can't hear or see them, but I can hear and see them just fine. *I think we should pull the plug* my dead grandfather says. *But I'm perfectly alive* I say. Then the woman from earlier crashes into the hospital room through the window. No one can see this happen but me. She is naked except for a tiny red cape. Her breasts are the smothering kind. Her thighs are an insatiable vibrating death.

THE ONE ABOUT THE ROBBERS

You tell me a joke about two robbers who hide from the police. One robber hides as a sack of cats and the other robber hides as a sack of potatoes. That is the punch line somehow, the sack of potatoes, but all I can think about is how my dad used to throw me over his shoulder when I was very small and call me his sack of potatoes. *I've got a sack of potatoes* he would yell, spinning around in a circle, the arm not holding me reaching out for a sale. *Does anyone want to buy my sack of potatoes?* No one ever wanted to buy me. We were always the only two people in the room.

THE DONUT HAWK

On a long hunt over the ridge, I finally spot the elusive hawk that is made of a donut. It is called the Donut Hawk. It has been a myth in my clan for generations, so I set out to prove its existence, and shoot at it. My first bullet goes right through its donut hole. It lifts off the ground clumsily, wet with sugary glaze, so I shoot again, killing it. When I approach it to bring its donut back to my village, I find that it is not the only donut hawk in existence, that in fact there are millions of donut hawks sleeping peacefully in a hidden valley on the other side of the ridge, each in perfect families of twelve. With my rifle, I kill one whole family. This is where donuts come from.

DON'T STEP ON THE FROG

The sign at Frog Lake says *Please Don't Step on the Frog*. I spend all day looking for the frog underneath the reeds, between the cattails at the edge of the water. I feel like I am constantly stepping on the frog, but I'm not. I don't think there is a frog, at least not anymore.

AFTER TAKING OUT THE GARBAGE FOR THE FIRST TIME

When I took out the garbage for the first time, my parents were proud, watching me from the living room window. I lifted the lid and then sealed it just like I was taught, drug the can a few feet from the curb. The garbage truck came, and the man smiled at me and flipped the bill of my baseball cap. During the walk back to the house, I felt like a different boy. All my parts died and were reborn. The house was miles away and looked like the kind of house a spider would live in. The walk took hours. When I got back, all the doors were locked. I could see through the living room window that my little sister was feeding the cat, her first chore too—but we didn't have a cat, and I didn't have a sister. I knocked and knocked on the window, but my parents never heard any of it. In the future, it's Christmas in Tierra del Fuego and all the villagers are dead. I am touching my body like a jellyfish in a giant mirror.

THE SEARCH

My mother was lost in the mall for three days.
Everyone was sure she was dead. My father, uncle
and I searched for her with a pack of search dogs.
Our plan was to track her scent, but we only
searched deep in the store that makes giant cookies
for special occasions, and writes custom messages
on them with frosting. On Valentines Day, they will
even make you a giant heart.

FISHING FOR STINGRAYS

I am on a fishing boat with a master stingray fisherman miles off the coast of Mexico Beach, but I have to be at the coffee shop where I work at 10. It is 9:45. *I have to go. I'm sorry, but I am going to be fired* I tell him. *There is time* he says, and we start putting jellyfish bait on strings and throwing them into the ocean. *These are just Ziploc bags filled with water* I say. *No they're not* he says. We were silent on the flat water for a few minutes, the sun dangling like a broken arm. Then we pulled out the same long wet string of Ziploc bags, hand over hand into the boat, our backs arched and aching. *One of my best catches of stingrays yet* he says. If I put a hole in this boat, he would never, even eventually, know. If my face were made of paper, he would draw on it his face, not looking into the distance.

I CLIMBED A MOUNTAIN AND FUCKED IT INTO THE SEA

I climbed a mountain and fucked it into the sea. I fucked the icebergs into the sky. I fucked the ships back into the trees, and I fucked the people on the ships back into the burnt-out caves. I fucked your father into orbit around some other sun, and your mother back into your grandmother's young arms. Then I fucked us deep into the future and we found your cat there. It looked happy.

HANDS

Four red hands float in the shittiness. The air is giving out. Horses jump over us, their hooves denting in our heads. When we look down, we do not have our hands. They've been replaced by something we've come to recognize as our parents.

COSTA RICA

With the money we get for the couch, we buy a little
house on the beach. There is no couch inside. We
buy our couch back, but have to sell the house to
do it. This cycle is how we keep on living. We never
grow poor, and we never age. We never really get to
know each other. We find some cats and they die
in a series of shivery fits, right in front of us, as if
to congratulate us on being human.

BUILDING OF UNSEEN CATS

When I woke up, it was the middle of the night and my building was on fire. The hallway was not filled with smoke, and then quickly it was. I rescued a few older men from their bathtubs, a few babies from their cribs. Outside, the air was filled with hair. Everyone but me was holding a plastic cage with a cat in it. We weren't supposed to have cats in my building, but there they all were, an invisible nation suddenly uncurtained into a blinding and brutal world. Everyone looked at me with a face that said *let's never speak of this.* Let's not look directly at what is meant to be loved in secret. Let's, for example, imagine the sea is always, constantly, and forever spilling toward us, that our screaming building is something worth escaping.

THE KILLING TREES

There is one tree for every person, and the trees have all started falling on the person they've grown tall to fall on, crushing their people's skulls into the ground. I take a train to the forest and stand before the tallest tree. *It's time* I tell it, but it keeps standing. When I try chopping it down, a cloud falls on me, and then a burning airplane, and then my mother and father, and then more burning airplanes.

NEIGHBORHOOD PLAGUE

My neighbors have been dying, one after the other in a row, each day, from east to west. You told me that if I didn't want to end up dead like my neighbors, that I should keep moving west. That seems like the last direction I'd want to move in.

LEAVING THE HOUSE

I leave the house for the first time. Or, more accurately, the house rots away from around me. The sun is blinding. My parents look young and happy in the sand. Or they look relieved. They are playing volleyball, just the two of them, and they are doing the opposite of what you would think good volleyball players should do, working together to keep the ball in the air. There is nothing special about them. By this I mean we spill out of their bodies, and then they don't take enough photographs, and then their bodies climb down a very tall ladder into a dark secret door just as they promised.

I AM THE DEAD PERSON
INSIDE ME

I am the dead person inside me. I am no smaller
than myself, no less papery. I breathe once and
teeth come out. On my second breath, I am
hunched into an incorrect shape. There is a
monster in the trees guessing at my name. And now
I'm sure of only nothing.

CASTING OUT THE KING OF BOYS

On my last day as king, I watched a dirty movie behind the couch. My father said I should get used to that sort of thing. I ate every last possible meal in the refrigerator. Those were great memories from someone exactly like me's childhood. Now I am in a field, I am part of the field, like a poppy, in my pretty dress. There is nothing larger to grow into.

WHAT I DID WITH THE ROCK

I was alone on the beach when I picked up a rock. I gave it a name and then I stood at the water with the rock in my hand. I gave it your name. It felt right—warm and cold at the same time—but I threw it as far as I could, and never saw it splash. *What have I done?* I asked. I stood there waiting for the rock to wash up. About 14,000 days later I died.

THE RECKONER

I am walking through a series of doors. On the other side of most doors is the same empty red room, but one door opens up to a room that is actually a field of heather, and another to the same room that is actually a field of heather full of dying dried-out swans. One room is loud with the baby versions of all the people I've ever loved and one room is silent with their ghosts. A dark hallway leads me to the last door. On the other side is a mountain town. The air is clean and cold. I can hear the ice breaking in the distance. There is a woman in a long black dress and a black scarf over her face. *Welcome to Spitzbergen* she says. Then she lifts up her dress. Nothing happens next.

INDEX

Airplanes, burning, 19, 51

Arms, or armlessness, or legs, 4, 14, 18, 29, 35, 41, 46, 47

Asking for help, 1, 8-11, 13, 18, 27-29, 32

Babies, or being handed a baby, 10, 11, 18, 33, 34, 50, 57

Balloon, red, (see also Red), 4, 22

Barbara, someone named, 21, 38

Bed, 8, 16, 19, 22, 25, 32

Beauty, 17, 14, 15, 25

Birth, or thawing, 1, 2, 6, 8, 44

Blood, 1, 7, 10, 15, 18, 23, 26-28, 35

Blood in the trees, 7, 11

Boats, or ships, 6, 17, 21, 46, 47

Bodies of water, specifically lakes, ponds, and rivers (see also Ocean), 4, 10, 12, 21, 30, 43, 46, 47, 50, 56

Boy, 6, 9, 44, 55

Cats, 41, 44, 47, 49, 50

Death, or imminent Death, or living forever, (see also Fjords, Killing), 1, 5, 4-11, 14-20, 23-27, 30, 32, 34, 39, 40, 44, 45, 48-52, 54, 56, 57

Dog, or the act of walking the dog, 1, 9, 21, 45

Doors, the act of knocking on the door, 16, 28, 44, 53, 57

Eyes, 11-13, 16, 18, 23, 26, 28, 31, 35

Faces, 3, 29, 46, 50, 57

Falling in love, 3, 4, 7, 11-16, 19, 24, 31, 35, 40

Falling from the sky, 19, 36, 38, 51

Father, or grandfather, 6, 9, 18, 33, 40, 41, 45-47, 51, 55

Fire, 20, 22, 50, 51

Fists, 13, 16

Flowers, bouquet of, 11, 16

French, or speaking French, 11, 12, 19

Fjords (see also Spitzbergen, Death), 1, 5

Future, the, 12, 20, 33, 45, 47

Glass, 3, 8, 10, 18

Grocery Store, 1, 18, 22

Hands, holding or falling off, 6, 7, 24, 26, 33, 36, 46, 48, 56

House, or home, 9, 16, 26, 32, 37, 44, 49, 53

Hospitals, or ambulances, 1, 8, 14, 26, 40

Killing, or the act of waiting for a killing, 1, 2, 8, 11, 14-18, 20, 22-26, 32, 40, 42, 48, 51, 52

Line (of customers), 21, 27

Microscopic, the idea of being, or the idea of being gigantic, 16, 37, 40, 44, 45

Money, indirect references to the exchange of, 12, 18, 21-23, 27, 41, 46, 49

Mouths, 9, 19, 39

Mountains, or cliffs, 2, 17, 25, 29, 47, 57

Neighborhood, 1, 52

Ocean, Arctic, 6

Ocean, regular, 7, 8

Pants, 18, 24

Paris (see also French), 11, 21, 22

Ponies or horses jumping over something, 30, 48

Red, 4, 18, 22, 40, 48, 57

Refrigerators, 28, 29, 55

Saving someone, the idea of, 11, 14, 23, 24, 26, 50

Screaming, 9, 50

Sexual Intercourse, or sexual activity, 21, 25, 35, 40, 47

Shirts, dress, 23, 24

Silence, or inability to hear, 2, 9, 18, 40, 44, 46, 57

Sleeping (see also Fakeness), 5, 9, 42

Spitzbergen, 2, 57

Strawberries (see also Throwing), 3, 17

Swans, 12, 14, 17, 57

Things coming out of other things, 8, 10, 29, 34, 39, 46, 50, 53, 54

Throwing, 3, 4, 17, 41, 46, 56

Trees (see also Blood in the trees), hovering in the trees, 1, 4, 17, 29, 32, 36, 37, 40, 47, 51, 54

Truth, 15, 16, 19, 25. 28, 43, 46, 50

Waking up inside of, 11, 18, 19, 50

Walking away, or into, 12, 16, 21, 24, 31, 32, 44, 57

Windows, looking out of or jumping out of, 8, 9, 16, 18, 23, 25, 40, 44

World, the, 8, 13, 15, 24, 26, 35, 36, 39, 50